Written by

Admiral Lord Nelson

Jarrold Colour Publications: Norwich

Boyhood Days

Six admirals carried the coffin to its last resting-place. Seven royal dukes, another twenty-five admirals and a hundred captains in full dress attended the state funeral on 9 January 1806. This was a national day of mourning and the deep sense of loss was felt by the whole country. Thousands of men and women lined the route to St Paul's to pay their last respects. London had never seen anything quite like this before.

Yet there were no such portents of greatness on 29 September 1758 when the wife of the Rector of Burnham Thorpe in Norfolk gave birth to her sixth child and fifth son. Both parents came of good stock and Mrs Nelson persuaded her relative, the second Baron Walpole, to act as godfather and give his name of Horatio to her baby. The christening took place on 15 November, but as the parish registers show that he had been privately baptised on 9 October there are grounds for thinking that Horatio was a sickly child. He certainly doted on his mother, and her death when he was but a boy of nine was a grievous hurt, the scar of which he was to carry all his life. He needed a mother for he was of poor physique and over-sensitive, yet he was engaged in one of the most arduous professions imaginable. When he was grown into manhood he was to find one. She was Emma, Lady Hamilton, a woman of extraordinary sexual attraction prepared to be not only mother but mistress as well. He found her irresistible. This passion was to cause distress to his friends, provide fodder for every cartoonist in London and threaten to ruin his career. Yet Nelson was for ever happy with his darling Emma.

His early boyhood years were happy ones. The Nelsons were by no means poor and Nelson's father was not only a churchman of unquestioning faith but also a scholar and a farmer.

Horatio went to school at Norwich and then to Downham Market where he persuaded the small boys at school to work the village pump so that he could sail paper boats in the resultant stream of water. Finally, after a spell at Paston Grammar School at North Walsham, his schooldays came to an end when he was but twelve years old.

This was a direct consequence of Edmund

Nelson's inability to bring up a family of eight on his own. His wife was sorely missed and there were no female relations at hand to help. He now turned to his brother-in-law, Maurice Suckling, who had fought with distinction in the Seven Years War and achieved the rank of senior captain. He was typical of the British naval officer at his very best – always a gentleman but a professional to his fingertips. He readily agreed that Horatio should go to sea with him as a midshipman merely remarking in that bluff way of his: 'What has poor Horatio done, who is so weak that he, above all the rest, should be sent to rough it out at sea? But let him come and the first time we go into action a cannon ball may knock off his head and provide for him at once.' Horatio was delighted – his uncle was already something of a hero – and he set off for Chatham in March 1771 to join Suckling's ship *Raisonnable*.

1 *left* The Reverend Edmund Nelson, destined to be the father of the greatest admiral the world has ever known, was the Rector of Burnham Thorpe, a tiny Norfolk village. The church was extensively restored in 1890 as a memorial to that same national hero, Horatio, Lord Nelson.
2 *below top* Horatio Nelson, carrying a flag in the foreground, was born in the Parsonage House at Burnham Thorpe. The painting is by F. Pocock. The house is now demolished.
3 *below bottom* Nelson's classroom at Paston Grammar School, North Walsham.

4 *above* Horatio Nelson had always adored and hero-worshipped his uncle, Captain Maurice Suckling, a professional sailor of courage and ability. In an age when promotion depended as much upon social influence as ability, he was indeed a most suitable mentor for a young man eager to make his way in the Royal Navy. This portrait was painted by T. Bardwell in 1764.

5 *right* Nelson was a midshipman by the time he was fifteen. The painter of this portrait is unknown, but at this age Nelson preferred to be known as Horace rather than Horatio.

Learning the Ropes

His nautical education now began in earnest. Elementary seamanship, the rudiments of navigation, the handling of ships' boats, the rigging of a ship of the line – all found places in his studies and he proved an avid pupil. So much so that after a few months aboard the *Raisonnable* Suckling considered that it was time for Horatio to put his new-found knowledge to the test by undertaking a long voyage to the West Indies in a merchantman.

After more than a year at sea Nelson returned home with more than confidence in his abilities as a seaman. Now he understood and could sympathise with the seamen who worked the ship. In later years this ability and his common humanity did much to make him the darling of the fleet. But first there was a spell of duty aboard his uncle's new ship *Triumph* on station at the mouth of the Thames.

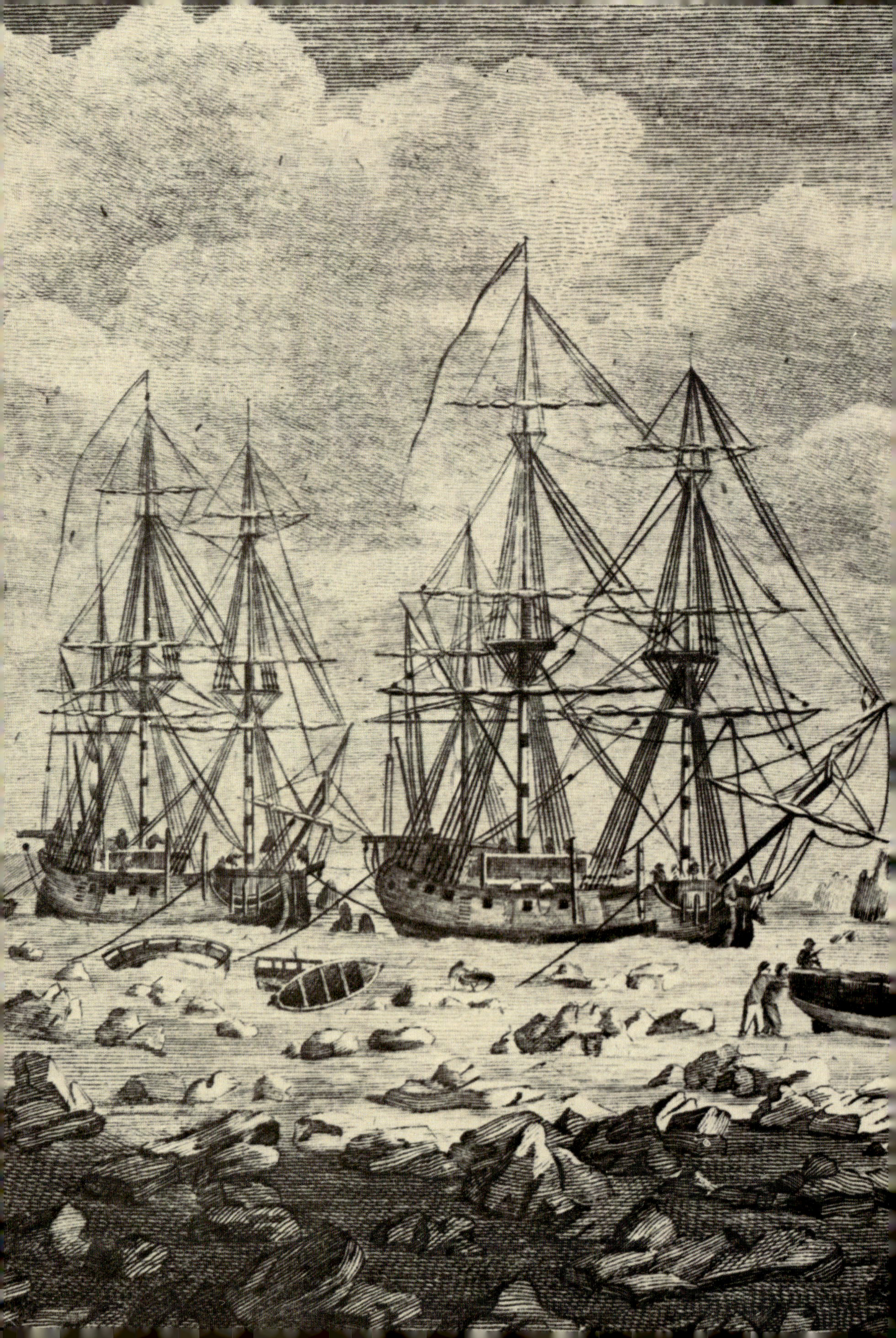

Nelson was barely fourteen years old yet he was entrusted with the command of *Triumph*'s tender plying between the Nore and the Pool of London. It was then that he mastered the tricky arts of navigation which he was to put to good use at Aboukir Bay and Copenhagen.

On 4 June 1773 Nelson joined *Carcass* as coxswain of the Captain's gig. She, with her companion *Racehorse*, was voyaging into the Arctic in search of a North-east Passage. The expedition was a failure scientifically but Nelson enjoyed every minute of it. Once when the ships were trapped in the ice some ten degrees from the pole, Nelson encountered a polar bear. Boy-like, he needs must have its skin for a trophy. Unfortunately his musket jammed. Not one whit abashed he charged and attempted to club the animal with the butt. The Captain of *Carcass* fearing a tragedy fired a signal gun. The bear loped off and the dejected but unrepentant boy returned to the ship protesting, 'Sir, I wanted to kill the bear that I might carry the skin to my father.'

6 This engraving of *Racehorse* and *Carcass* trapped in the polar ice in latitude 80 degrees 37 minutes, first appeared in volume 5 of *Payne's Universal Geography*. At this time Nelson was captain's coxswain aboard *Carcass* and although this voyage of discovery accomplished little he thoroughly enjoyed it.

Nelson next transferred to *Seahorse* and now not only took part in a naval engagement but experienced for the first time the harshness of naval discipline. In under two years he witnessed over 200 floggings. Then he contracted a tropical fever and was ordered home. He was now at the cross-roads of his career. Overcome with melancholy he not only doubted his abilities but cared little whether he lived or died. The mood passed and was replaced with a glow of patriotism which was soon to become a fire. Nelson made up his mind there and then that he would become a hero.

In April, when restored to health, he was posted to the frigate *Lowestoffe* commanded by Captain William Locker who was to become his friend and mentor. The American War of Independence was now in full swing and *Lowestoffe* was engaged in escorting ships to the West Indies.

Nelson was now eighteen and after two years' service in the West Indies had gained a considerable reputation as a young officer of promise. On 11 June 1779 he was appointed post-captain. His future was now assured, for not only was he qualified to command the largest ships of the line but, as his length of service increased, only death or disablement could prevent him from becoming an admiral.

Long before then, however, he was given command of the frigate *Hinchingbrooke* and ordered to take part in the amphibious campaign against the Spaniards in

7 Detail from a portrait of Captain William Locker by G. Stuart.

8 *right* Horatio Nelson aged eighteen years by J. F. Rigaud.

Capt. Horatio Nelson

Nicaragua. The campaign although successful was ill conceived and the troops badly equipped for jungle warfare. Yellow fever took its toll and only ten men survived of the *Hinchingbrooke*'s complement of 200. Nelson covered himself with glory but was ordered home suffering from dysentery. On 23 August 1781, after a short stay at Burnham Thorpe, he once more sailed, for North America this time in command of the frigate *Albemarle*.

At the end of the war Nelson, when on holiday in France, met Miss Andrews and fell violently in love. Mary Simpson had aroused similar emotions in him in Quebec, but so convinced was he that this time it was the 'real thing' that he asked his uncle for an allowance so that he could propose marriage. The lady refused him. There was little time to mope for on 18 March he was again ordered to the West Indies – this time as captain of the frigate *Boreas*. He had a thankless task. The Americans were still trading with the islanders as if they still enjoyed British citizenship. He had to stop this. Nelson soon ran foul of everyone and was frustrated at every turn. Then he met Frances Nisbet, the widow of a doctor with a five-year-old son, living on Nevis. After a two-year courtship they were married in 1787 and shortly afterwards Nelson sailed for home. He arrived on 4 July and found himself far from popular with the Admiralty. On 30 November the crew of *Boreas* were paid off and her captain placed on half-pay of £50 per year. Economics decreed that the young couple settle in Parsonage House at Burnham Thorpe.

9 *below* This portrait of Frances, Viscountess Nelson, was painted when she was forty years of age. Nelson married Frances, then a widow, at Nevis on 11 March 1787. Prince William Henry was among the guests.
10 *right* Sir William Hamilton, painted by an unknown artist in Naples in 1777. Sir William, born in 1730, was the grandson of the Duke of Hamilton.

The Mediterranean and Emma Hamilton

Nelson spent the next six years kicking his heels in Norfolk. Each request for a ship was coldly refused, then on 30 January 1793 he was given command of *Agamemnon*. She was a good, well-manned ship and it was a very happy crew that sailed to join Lord Hood in the Mediterranean two months after the revolutionaries of France had declared war.

Toulon remained loyal to the monarchy and Hood had reinforced the garrison with sailors and marines in an attempt to halt the rebel advance. But more help was needed and Nelson was dispatched to Naples to gain the support of King Ferdinand IV. His contact was the British Ambassador, Sir William Hamilton. He was about sixty-three, a sophisticated aristocrat and classical scholar of repute. His wife, Emma, thirty years his junior, had lived with Sir William for five years but had been the legal Lady Hamilton for only two. She made an instant impression on Nelson but there is no hint in his letters that he had met the love of his life.

Her background was vastly different from Nelson's for she came of humble folk and had reached the fringes of society under the protection of Sir Henry Featherstonhaugh and when he tired of her she lived for several years with Charles Greville. She was heartbroken when Greville passed her over to his uncle Sir William Hamilton, who was seeking a lively young wife to fit in with the permissive society of Naples. He certainly got more than he bargained for. Gradually Emma's powerful personality swamped him. She became the confidante of the Queen and a political force to be reckoned with.

With Emma's help Nelson's mission was successfully completed and he set sail for Sardinia where he fought a squadron of French frigates single-handed. But the situation at Toulon worsened and despite reinforcements from Naples the town had to be evacuated. Unfortunately the operation was bungled and eighteen monarchist ships which should have joined Hood were captured. Five years were to pass before Nelson finally destroyed them.

Hood now needed a base from which to direct operations and Corsica seemed an obvious choice. The French occupying forces were firmly established in the island's many walled towns and had to be winkled out one by one. At first Nelson, like most of his men, found the campaign ashore a welcome change but high summer brought with it the familiar mix of dysentery, skin diseases, exhaustion, fever, and a host of minor epidemics. Then on 12 July 1794 while supervising a battery at Calvi Nelson was struck by a splinter and lost the sight of his right eye. That same October Hood, now a very sick man, was replaced by Admiral Hotham, an affable enough man but lacking the dash needed to carry the war to the enemy.

Eventually on 13 March seventeen French ships ventured out of Toulon in an attempt to retake Corsica but when intercepted by a force of but fourteen British ships they attempted to run for it. They would have escaped too had not Ça Ira fouled another ship and become partially dismasted. A frigate which bravely attacked her was soon driven off by two huge French vessels who then took Ça Ira in tow.

Nelson in *Agamemnon* was far ahead of the rest of the fleet when he came up with the damaged ship. He immediately attacked and poured broadside after broadside into the Ça Ira. When she finally struck her colours she had 400 dead and wounded to

11 *left* In Emma Hamilton, George Romney, the celebrated portrait painter, found the perfect model and he painted her over and over again. She also sat for Hoppner, Lawrence and Schmidt.
12 *below* The British fleet drawn up in Naples Bay with Vesuvius in the background, is a detail from a picture by Guardi. It was in Naples that Nelson met Lady Hamilton for the first time, and with her help succeeded in persuading Ferdinand IV to oppose the revolutionaries of France.

Nelson's 12. Another enemy vessel was also captured but the rest escaped. Hotham was well satisfied but Nelson was far from pleased. A golden opportunity to destroy the French fleet had been lost.

Nevertheless this action established Nelson's reputation as a fighting captain. Tales of his daring were on every lip and he was promoted to the prestigious rank of Colonel of Marines. Then to Nelson's delight that old sea-dog Sir John Jervis was appointed Admiral of the Fleet. He was not only an experienced admiral but also a commander of vision. It was he who first appreciated Nelson's potential and almost his first act was to promote him to the rank of commodore. The *Agamemnon*, however, was now in a parlous state and Nelson transferred to *Captain*, a third-rater of seventy-four guns.

The war continued to go badly for the British and with the collapse of Spain not only had Gibraltar to be evacuated but erstwhile friends became foes overnight. It was while taking part in this operation in *Le Minerve* that Nelson, by magnificent seamanship and intrepid daring, saved Lieutenant Thomas Hardy from the Spaniards and clinched a lifelong friendship.

Cape St Vincent

When Nelson, once again in *Captain*, joined the main fleet off Cape St Vincent on 14 February a major battle was inevitable. With only fifteen ships of the line to the enemy's twenty-seven Jervis knew that victory could not be won by the conventional exchange of broadsides while sailing on parallel courses. A bold tactical plan was needed. Noticing that the Spanish fleet was in two groups he decided to sail between them and destroy the first squadron before the second could arrive. Once through the gap the British were to go about in succession and then attack. The tactics were sound but the timing was awry. It was obvious to Nelson, last but two in the line, that the Spanish fleet would be united in a single line of battle long before action could be joined. All seemed lost but Nelson took his ship out of line, the most serious crime he could commit, and hurled himself through the rapidly closing gap and immediately engaged seven of the enemy. Fortunately Jervis understood Nelson's tactic and as *Captain* disappeared

13 *left* This watercolour by Nicholas Pocock shows Nelson in command of *Agamemnon* raking the dismasted Frenchman *Ça Ira*.
14 *above* Nelson receiving the sword of the Spanish admiral on the quarterdeck of *San Josef* after he had boarded and captured her at St Vincent. The original painting is by D. Orme.
15 *below* Nelson was almost captured off Cadiz, being beaten back only after a ferocious hand-to-hand battle.

in clouds of gun-smoke he ordered Collingwood and Troubridge to go to his assistance while the rest of the fleet slowly came up astern.

Captain was soon immobilised but, not one whit deterred, Nelson decided not only to board the nearest ship, *San Nicolas*, but to lead the boarding-party himself. They soon gained control of the upper deck but as they fought their way below *San Josef* came alongside and opened fire. Nelson's men were at her in an instant and such was the fury of their onslaught that she immediately surrendered. Later, on the deck of *San Nicolas* Nelson received the swords of both vanquished captains. Needless to say such a spectacular feat of arms made Nelson the toast of London. He was presented with a knighthood and promoted Rear-Admiral of the Blue.

But this triumph was followed by anti-climax. On 3 July he was nearly captured by a Spanish gunboat off Cadiz and then there was the disaster of Teneriffe. Two hundred men were lost in that ill-starred attack on Santa Cruz and Nelson himself, wounded by grape-shot, had his right arm amputated.

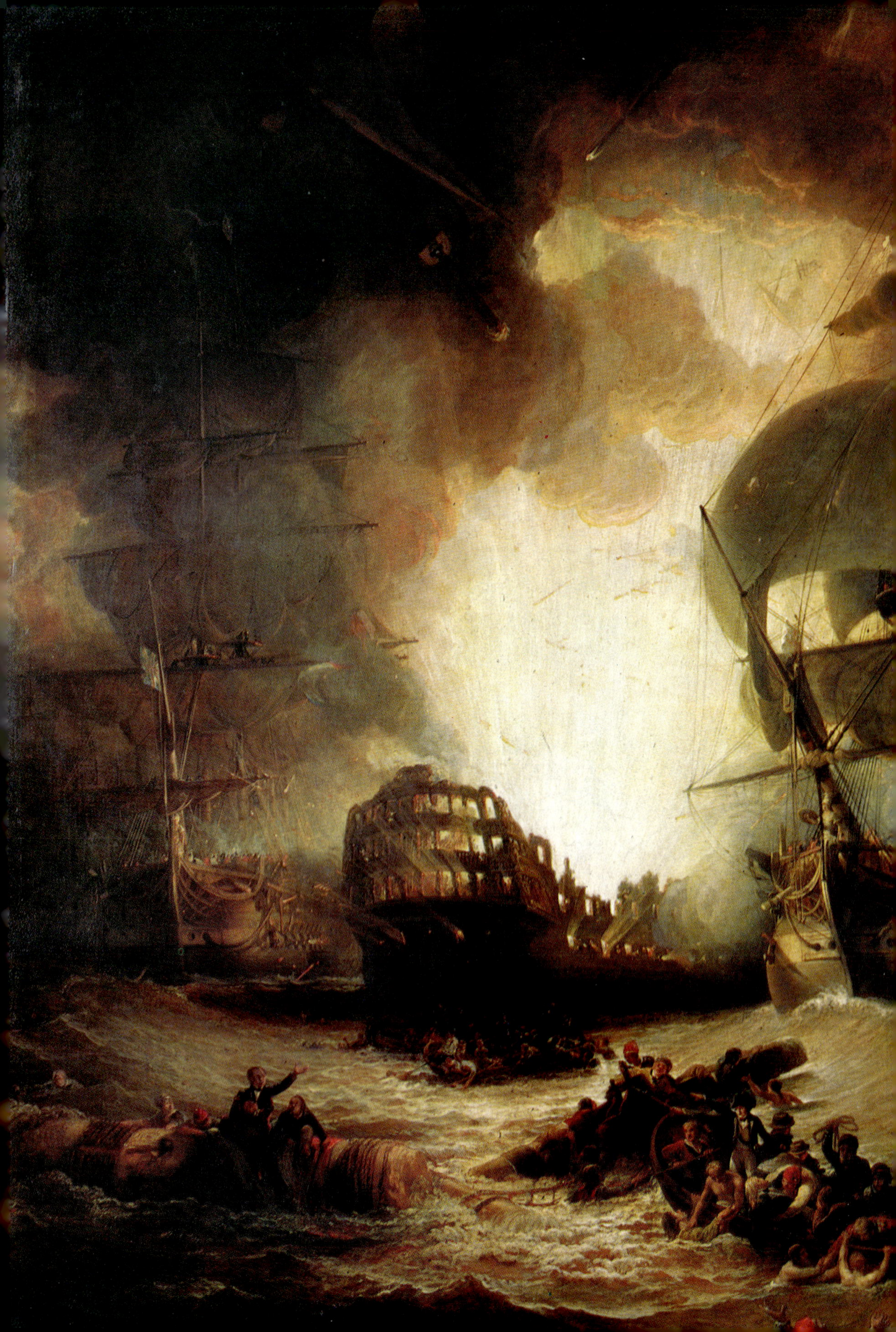

16 At the height of the Battle of the Nile, *L'Orient*, the French flagship and pride of the fleet, explodes. The fighting stops for a while and then continues with unabated fury.

Battle of the Nile and Emma again

Seven months later, his arm completely healed, he was once more on his way to the Mediterranean to join Admiral Jervis, now Earl St Vincent.

Nelson's task was to blockade the port and prevent the French from joining the Spaniards in Cadiz. Then after weeks of waiting a north-westerly gale sprang up and blew the blockade off station. The French were away in a trice with Nelson in pursuit. It was 1 August 1798 before he came up with them and then they were drawn up in a seemingly impregnable position across Aboukir Bay just off Alexandria. The thirteen ships of the line, supported by guns ashore, were anchored in a slight curve with their flanks protected by shoals.

Nelson attacked at once. Captain Foley in *Goliath* boldly sailed round the French line and attacked from the unprotected landward side. Four more ships followed and the destruction of the French fleet, caught in the resultant cross-fire, was inevitable. Only two French ships of the line and two frigates survived. Napoleon had lost not only his entire fleet but more than 5,000 men and was trapped in Egypt.

There was now nothing to fear from the French in the Mediterranean. Nelson's ships needed repairing and it seemed sensible to sail for Naples the centre of resistance in Europe. Then too Lady Hamilton was there.

She it was who insisted that Nelson should stay in her house. He was far from well. He had a recurrence of fever and a

17 *left* The start of the Battle of the Nile as seen by Nicholas Pocock. Captain Foley in *Goliath* is sailing round the French fleet which is at anchor head to wind.
18 *above* Part of the Brontë estate bestowed on Nelson by the King of Naples after his great victory. The estate brought in an annual income of £3,000.

throbbing head wound. Had he needed further persuasion then Emma Hamilton's indignation at the Government's refusal to make him a viscount would have tipped the scales. She flattered him outrageously, flirted with him, indulged him, and above all mothered him. She presided at his fortieth birthday party and Nelson found her irresistible.

Nelson's presence encouraged the King to raise an army and march on Rome. The French reaction was swift and predictable and the Neapolitan army was soon in headlong retreat. The fall of Naples became inevitable and Nelson, feeling that he had encouraged the King in his rashness, supervised the evacuation of the royal party to Palermo on 23 December.

The subsequent recapture of Naples by the royalists and the callous execution of the rebels reflects little credit on Nelson. A grateful King Ferdinand bestowed upon him the Dukedom of Brontë but his fortunes seemed to be on the wane.

In October 1799 Napoleon had escaped from Egypt, eluded the British blockade and arrived back in France. He still held Malta and the unsympathetic Lord Keith had replaced Earl St Vincent as Commander-in-Chief. When Nelson refused to obey an order to join him off Minorca, arguing that Naples was in the greater danger, his enemies maintained that it was Lady Hamilton who was keeping him there. He even took her aboard the *Foudroyant* in the hope that she might see the fall of Valletta.

The Admiralty had had enough. He was ordered home. But Nelson was in no hurry and decided on an overland journey which, beginning on 13 July, was to take four months. He was lionised in Vienna, Prague, Dresden, and Hamburg yet so besotted was he with Emma Hamilton that he frequently cut a ridiculous figure and embarrassed all his friends.

On 6 November 1800 Nelson landed at Yarmouth to receive a tumultuous welcome. His carriage was hauled by the multitude to the Wrestlers Inn where he received the freedom of the borough. Then once the boisterous celebrations were over, Nelson, escorted by cavalry, set off for London. Fanny, his wife, awaited him there. Her welcome was cool and restrained. It was an agonising time for Nelson. He had now to choose between two women – Fanny, well-bred, respected and admired by his friends, and Emma, the vulgar social climber and woman of easy virtue. His marriage lasted little more than another month, although it was not until March 1801 that he settled half his income on Fanny and insisted that their separation should be permanent. Needless to say the

affair was savagely lampooned by all the satirists and cartoonists of the day, but even they were unaware that Emma had given birth to Nelson's daughter Horatia on 1 February. It was one of history's best-kept secrets.

Copenhagen

Escape from this emotional turmoil came with his appointment as second-in-command to Sir Hyde Parker on an expedition to the Baltic. This had been occasioned by Tsar Paul of Russia. He was now in league with Napoleon and had revived the old alliance with Denmark, Norway, and Sweden. The British were determined to eliminate the threat before the French could gain control of their new allies' fleets. Nelson had a poor opinion of his senior officer, thinking him incompetent and lazy, but once on active service aboard *St George* his habitual good humour and calm detachment returned. Parker was every bit as cautious as Nelson had feared and anchored off the Kattegat while ambassadors were dispatched to Copenhagen to demand that Denmark withdraw from the alliance. Nelson chafed at the delay for he realised that not only was rejection of the ultimatum inevitable but that the enemy was being given time to concentrate his forces. He urged immediate attack but it was not until it was obvious that a pitched battle could not be avoided that he was given charge of the vessels of shallow draught, including twelve ships of the line, and given his head. Accordingly Nelson in *Elephant* sailed past Copenhagen and anchored to the south leaving Parker in his ships four miles away to the north. Nelson appreciating the strength of the enemy's position realised that there was no room for tactical brilliance and victory would go to the fleet which fought most efficiently. The action began disastrously for three of his ships ran aground but the other nine anchored against the Danes and were immediately hidden from view in clouds of smoke. Certainly Parker could see nothing. He felt the day to be lost and ordered the action to be broken off. When this was brought to his notice Nelson put the telescope to his blind eye and remarked that he could see no signal. An hour later victory belonged to the British. The Danes had lost 6,000 men but Nelson had been near to defeat for his ships could not have fought on much longer.

This, perhaps Nelson's most hard-fought victory, aroused no popular enthusiasm. The French were feared, the Danes were not; and although Nelson was made a Viscount he smarted at this lack of public recognition. He was, however, Commander-in-Chief for the first time and on 4 August launched an ambitious but unsuccessful attack on Boulogne. On 22 March 1802 peace was signed at Amiens.

19 *top left* Nelson landed on 6 November 1800 at this little jetty in Yarmouth nearly four months after he was ordered home by the Admiralty. His had been a triumphant progress across Europe, but he waited in vain in Hamburg for the frigate he was convinced the Admiralty would send to bring him back. Instead he was forced to sail from Cuxhaven in the mail packet *King George*. The warmth of his reception, however, soon banished all thoughts of pique and resentment.
20 *bottom left* Horatia, Nelson's illegitimate daughter begotten of Lady Hamilton on *Foudroyant* was born on 1 February 1801. The couple kept the birth secret and when writing about Horatia referred to her as having other parents. The father, Mr Thompson, was supposed to be a young officer serving with Nelson, while Emma pretended to be looking after Mrs Thompson and the child. They were thus able to exchange confidences about Horatia without revealing their true relationship. Horatia died not knowing that Nelson was her real father.
21 *overleaf* In 1801 Nelson was ordered to the Baltic to compel Denmark to break off her armed neutrality pact with Russia and Sweden. The Battle of Copenhagen was a hard-fought affair and Nelson had been near defeat before finally winning the day. This picture by Nicholas Pocock shows Nelson in *Elephant* moving his ships into position at the Battle of Copenhagen.

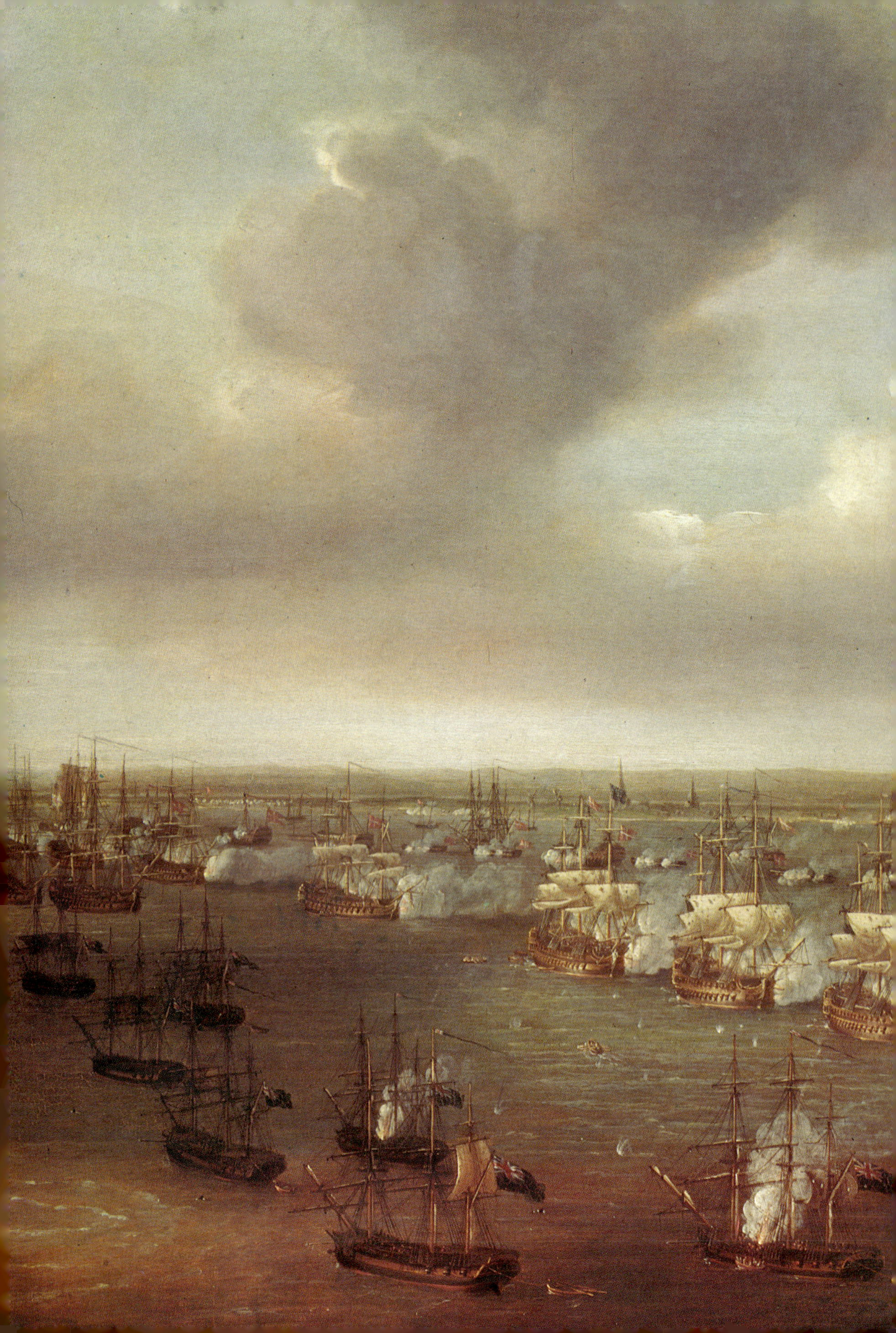

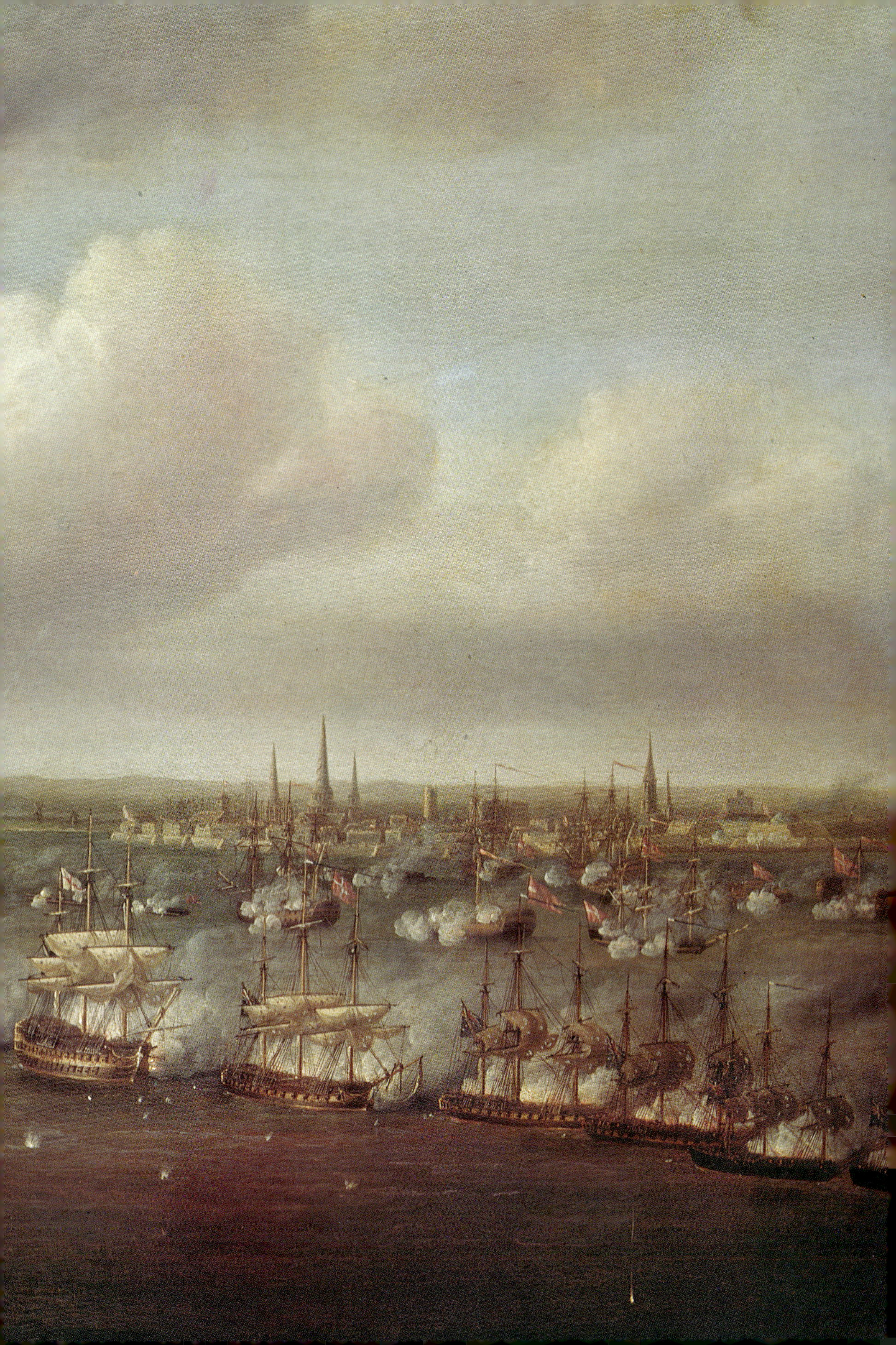

Victory at Trafalgar

Nelson retired to Merton, an elegant country house near Wimbledon, purchased at his behest by Emma. There he lived with the Hamiltons until the death of Sir William early in 1803. But this bucolic peace was not to last for Bonaparte was eager to resume his attempt to conquer Europe. In May Nelson hoisted his flag in *Victory* as Commander-in-Chief and set sail for the Mediterranean.

Once again the French fleet was imprisoned in Toulon. Many dull uneventful months of watching and waiting passed. To many the blockade seemed purposeless but it saved England. For Napoleon was now ready to invade. He intended the French and Spanish fleets to burst through the blockade and join forces in the West Indies. Then, after ravaging the islands, they would sweep across the Atlantic and destroy the British. Once in command of the Channel Napoleon could land upwards of 150,000 soldiers in England and the defeat of his old enemy would be assured.

The French commander, Admiral Pierre Villeneuve a veteran of Aboukir Bay, made one fruitless attempt to break out in January 1805 and then some three months later tried again. He passed into the

Atlantic with Nelson in hot pursuit. It was normal practice at times like these when the enemy's intentions were in doubt to concentrate off Ushant but Nelson would have none of it. He continued to pursue Villeneuve all round the West Indies and harried him to such effect that he abandoned his plans for a meeting with the Emperor's other squadrons and sailed back to Europe. Attempts to intercept him failed and he succeeded in joining the Spanish fleet in Cadiz. Nelson returned home to report that the end was now in sight.

On Sunday 15 September, after twenty-five days at Merton, he joined *Victory* at Portsmouth and thirteen days later was once more with the fleet. On

22 *bottom left* Nelson was a vain man, proud of his accomplishments. Portraits there are of him in profusion, but always he is in uniform and bedecked with decorations. Just one, this by Fuger painted in 1800, shows him in the unfamiliar garb of a civilian.

23 *centre* When Nelson hankered after a 'farm' Lady Hamilton purchased Merton Place, an elegant house with an attractive garden convenient to both the Admiralty and Portsmouth. When Nelson joined the Hamiltons in October 1802 he found at Merton not only a home but a constant reminder of his triumphs. Trophies and souvenirs were everywhere – the topmast of *L'Orient* stood in the hall – and the walls were bedecked with canvasses depicting his glorious victories and portraits of himself and his mistress. Needless to say he entertained both lavishly and extravagantly and Sir William began to protest, but the last thing he wanted was to be estranged from either Emma or Nelson. In the event the strange relationship between the three lasted until Sir William's death in 1803.

24 *bottom right* Detail from A. C. Gow's picture of Nelson embarking at Portsmouth to join *Victory*.

20 October Villeneuve, with eighteen French and fifteen Spanish ships of the line, left Cadiz and Nelson positioned his twenty-seven ships to cut off his escape. The British were in two columns, one led by Nelson the other by Collingwood in *Royal Sovereign*. As the leading ships came within range they were bound to be subjected to a withering concentration of fire but Nelson strode his quarterdeck and refused to change out of the distinctive uniform which made him such an obvious target. Then Nelson made his famous signal, 'England expects that every man will do his duty' – and when this was greeted with cheering followed it with his last instruction, 'Engage the enemy more closely.' Captain Hardy then steered *Victory* between the French flagship *Bucentaure* and *Redoutable* and raked the former from end to end. *Victory* then

25 *below* Monamy Swaine has painted *Victory* in the Mediterranean flying the flag of Vice-Admiral Hood. She had the reputation of being a good sea boat, had an armament of 104 guns and was designed to carry water and provisions for four months for a ship's company of 900 men. By modern standards the living conditions of the crew were unendurable yet the senior officers lived in style. Three o'clock dinner, for instance, invariably consisted of three main courses accompanied by suitable wines, a superb dessert, coffee and liqueurs. Yet Nelson ate sparingly and drank but little. He did, however, occupy three commodious cabins under the poop – a stateroom in which he worked with his secretaries, a reception area and a dining and sleeping cabin – and these three rooms together accounted for nearly a quarter of the upper deck. *Plan opposite p.1*
26 *top right*   The artist Davidson recaptures the excitement and bustle on the quarterdeck of the *Victory* as Nelson's famous signal 'England expects that every man will do his duty' flutters on the halyards. This signal was received on all sides with tremendous enthusiasm and then Nelson made what was to be his last signal, 'Engage the enemy more closely.' He left that flying.
27 *bottom right*   The first enemy shots at Trafalgar burst *Victory*'s fore topsail asunder, yet Nelson, wearing the undress uniform of a vice-admiral adorned with the stars of the four orders of chivalry to which he was entitled, remained on the quarterdeck despite the entreaties of Captain Hardy to go below.

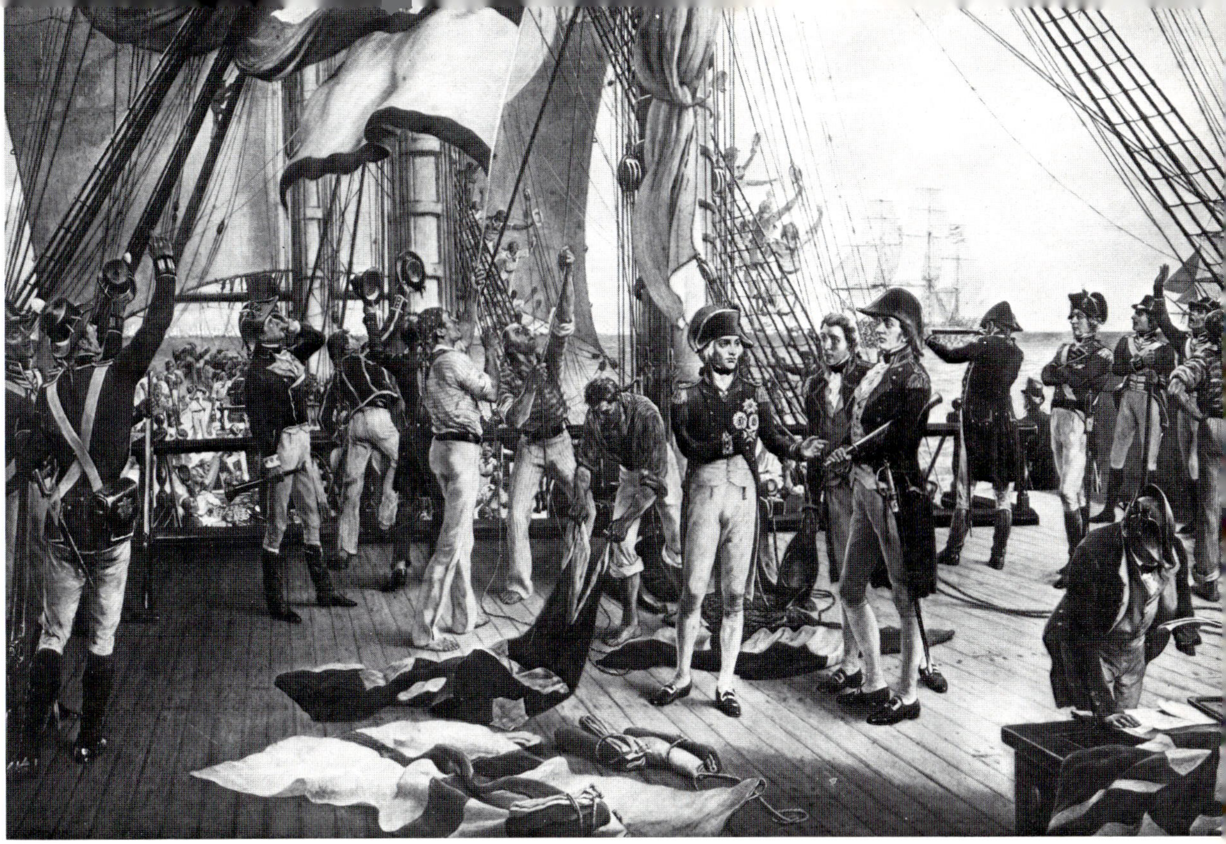

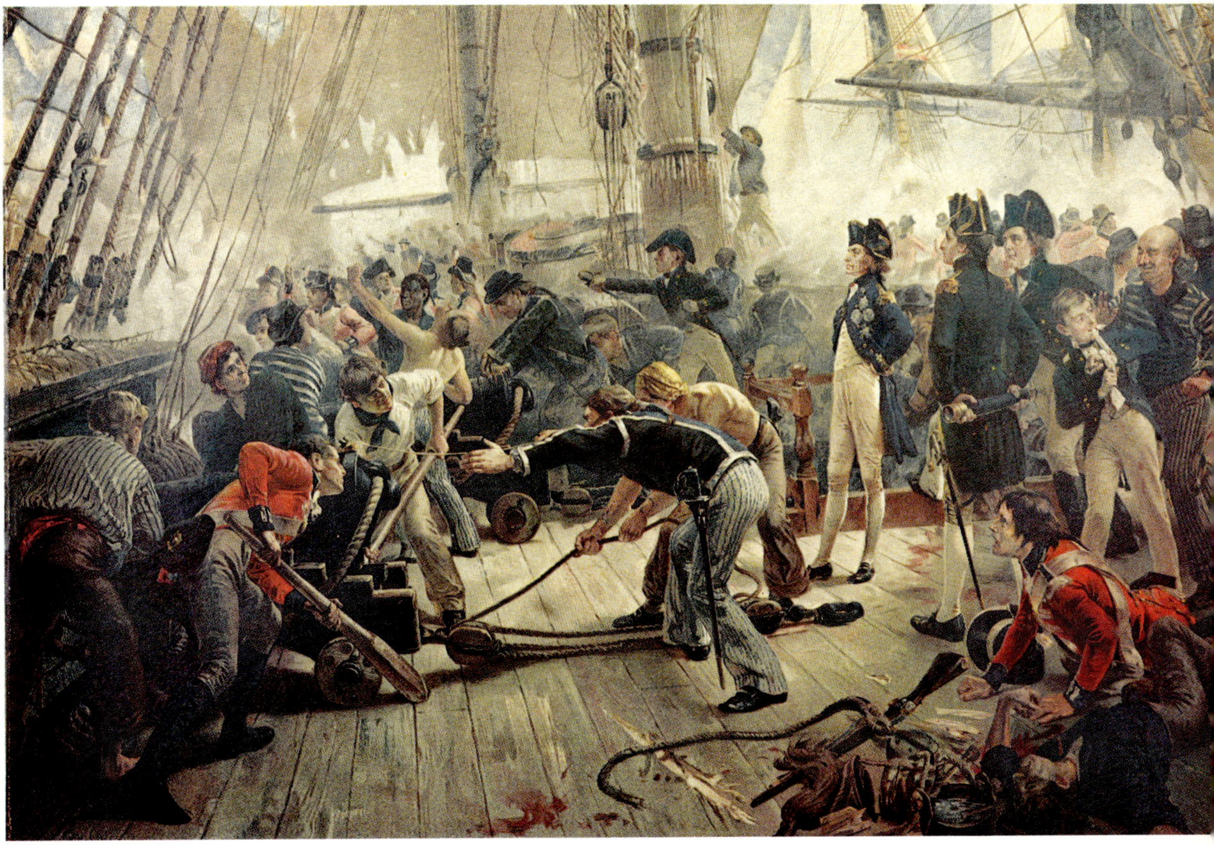

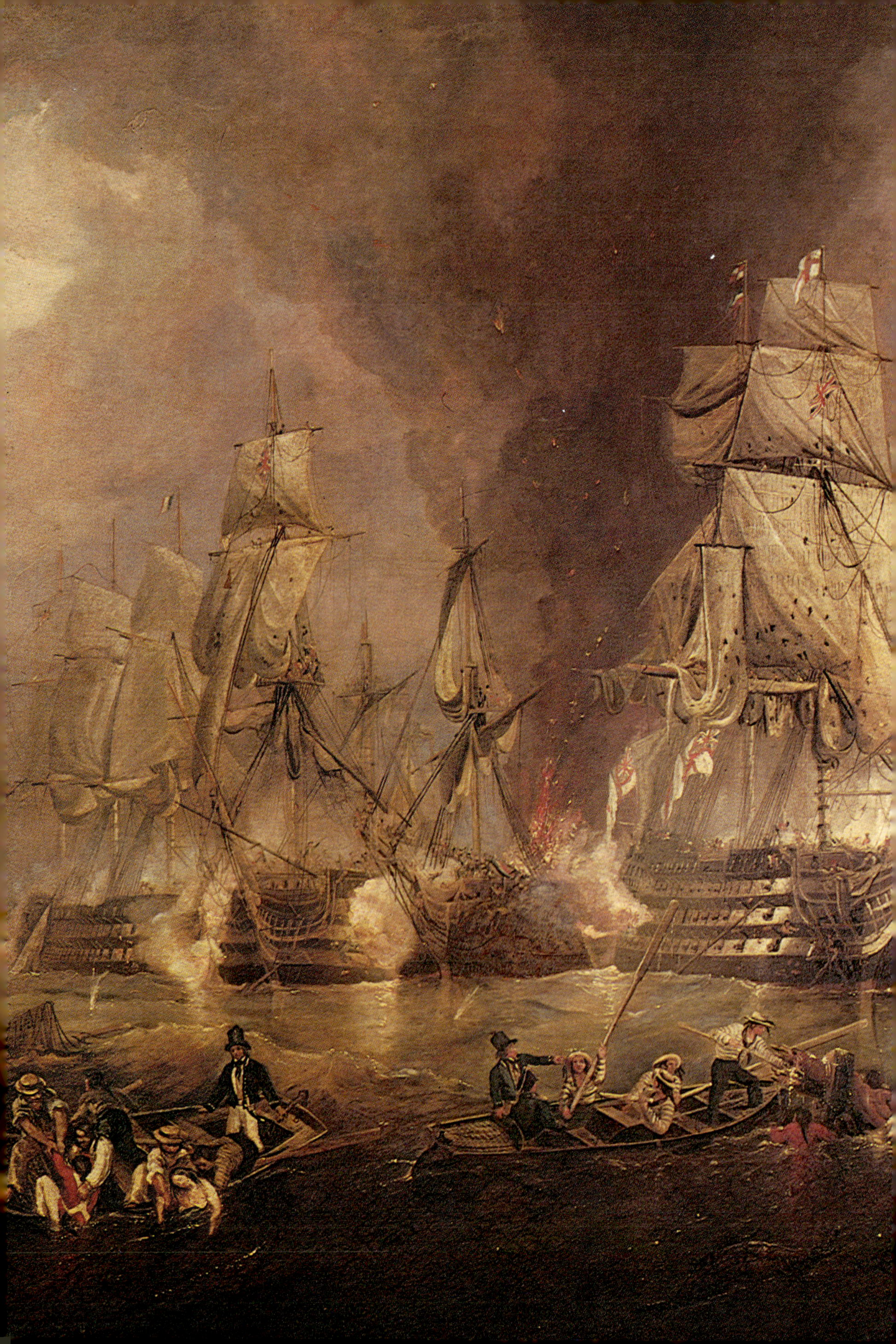

28 *left* The atmosphere of a sea battle at the time of Nelson is faithfully conveyed in this detail from an oil-painting of the Battle of Trafalgar.

29 *above* Captain Thomas Masterman Hardy, Nelson's lifelong friend and brother in arms in all his major victories.

collided with *Redoutable* and with their riggings entwined and their guns muzzle to muzzle the crews fought like tigers. After thirty minutes of fierce fighting Nelson was shot by a French sniper. As Nelson was carried below he covered his face with a handkerchief lest his crew be downhearted by this stroke of ill fortune. It was obvious that his end was near. His last thoughts were of Lady Hamilton and his daughter Horatia and he begged the nation to take care of them. Some three hours later he died knowing that victory was complete. Nineteen enemy ships had surrendered and not one British ship had been lost. This annihilation of the French ensured that Napoleon's dreams of an invasion were at an end and that British supremacy at sea

30 *previous page* As he was pacing the quarterdeck with Captain Hardy, Nelson was mortally wounded by a sniper positioned in the mizzen of *Redoutable*. The Admiral made an unmistakable target, and the musket shot passed through his shoulder and chest before lodging in the spine. The original picture was painted by Denis Dighton.

was not to be challenged again until 1914. Nelson's body was brought home in his flagship for the magnificent state funeral that followed. Yet his last wishes were entirely ignored. A grateful nation bestowed honour and riches on his parson brother and his estranged wife, but the woman who had meant so much to him was callously brushed aside. Emma, Lady Hamilton, died penniless some ten years later in Calais attended only by her daughter Horatia. Horatia married a clergyman, raised a large family, and then in her turn died at the age of eighty-one never knowing for certain that Nelson was her father. That was only proved years afterwards.

31 *below* The *Victory* her masts and rigging shot away being towed into Gibraltar after Trafalgar, from a painting by Clarkson Stanfield.